FRANK
LLOYD
WRIGHT

FRANK LLOYD WRIGHT

Thomas A. Heinz

With best wishes

ST. MARTIN'S PRESS
NEW YORK

Front cover
Hillside Home School, Spring Green, Wisconsin, 1902
remodeled 1932, view from the south.

Back cover
Nathan G. Moore House, Oak Park, 1895 rebuilt 1923.

Frontispiece
Frank Lloyd Wright House, Oak Park, 1895 playroom.

All of the colour photographs in this book were taken by the author.

For information write:
St. Martin's Press, Inc.
175 Fifth Avenue
New York, NY 10010

Library of Congress Catalog Card Number 81-48389
ISBN 0-312-30330-0 Cloth 0-312-30331-9 Paper

Printed and bound in Hong Kong

Contents

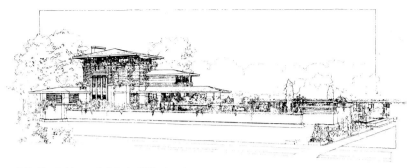

W.E. Martin House, Oak Park, 1903, elevation.

Introduction

This book does not attempt to be a photo essay on the complete work of Frank Lloyd Wright; indeed, many volumes would be necessary to document his prolific seventy-year career. Instead, these photos are offered as an overview of the incredible diversity of form and structure which is his legacy to us. From the houses of the 1890s, with their Sullivanesque detailing, to the revolutionary Robie House and Fallingwater; from the Prairie house (1900-1915) to the Usonian house (1936-1959), both of which were unique, unprecedented solutions to the needs of American families of the time; from the modest, compact design for Stephen M.B. Hunt to the magnificent, sprawling house for Susan Lawrence Dana, in which money was no object; from the hundreds of private residences to churches, office complexes, hotels, theatres, schools, and even a windmill and a gasoline filling station, Frank Lloyd Wright designed buildings that added new dimensions to architectural experience.

The books and articles written about Wright and his work number in the thousands.[1] They range from scholarly analyses to reminiscenses by family and clients, from general biographies to very specialized monographs. The architect himself was a prolific writer who began to expound his architectural theories and personal philosophy as early as 1901. A selected bibliography is included, and the reader seeking to expand his knowledge is urged to read the many fine works already published. However, there are several important points which are frequently overlooked that I would like to consider here.

THE PROCESS OF REFINEMENT

For Wright, achieving the best possible building was a continual process; never completely satisfied, he always re-evaluated his work and tried to improve upon it. This occurred not only in the initial design phases; Wright continued to alter his buildings during construction as well as after they were built. Years later, he even would alter drawings and photographs for publication in order to demonstrate his most current thinking. He was never really finished with a design but constantly refined and perfected it.

The Initial Design Phases

Like all architects, Wright often developed the designs of buildings before presenting them to the client and then usually modified them again based on additional information and input from the client. Unfortunately, multiple plans and studies for his buildings have not been widely published. *The Drawings of Frank Lloyd Wright,*[2] which is largely a compilation of perspective presentation drawings, contains many instances of such reworking and some valuable comparisons can be made: the Richard Lloyd-Jones House (Tulsa, 1929) was originally based on a triangular grid but was revised to a rectangular one; the cantilevers on the Calico Mills Building project (Ahmedabad, India, 1946) were modified; the grading of the site and the size of the car port of the Hanna House (Palo Alto, 1937) were significantly changed; the trellises of the Sturges House (Brentwood Heights, 1939) were considerably elongated; small but important changes were made in the wood detailing of the Rose Pauson House (Phoenix, 1939); and for the famous Guggenheim Museum (New York, 1956) there were no fewer than nine significant variations done over a period of fourteen years! These are but a few examples, and except for the Lloyd-Jones House and the Guggenheim Museum, they are fairly minor modifications. Because they are presentation drawings, they represent the culmination of many hours of design; seeing the drawings leading up to these would be instructive, indeed. Most of Wright's designs probably underwent development and refinement to varying degrees. As the thousands of drawings at Taliesin become more accessible to scholars, the true scope of this facet of his work will be more fully understood.

During and After Construction

What makes Wright unique is that he did not stop re-

W.E. Martin House, Oak Park, 1903.

Warren Hickox House, Kankakee, 1900.

designing his buildings once ground had been broken. Often he continued to improve his buildings while they were under construction. Seeing the spaces develop in three dimensions often gave him additional ideas. One documented instance of such a change is in the Willits House in Highland Park, Illinois (1902). In construction photographs, the second floor west wall of the south wing is in one plane, [3] but the house as it exists today is proof that this wall was re-located about three feet further west. This was an extremely significant alteration. As originally designed, the area would have been a rather normal looking stairhall, but the enlargement made it truly a 'great space'. After the very low (6'6") entry, the space virtually explodes to a full two stories and terminates in a superb art glass ceiling light and statue of the *Nike of Samothrace*. The scheme of a stairway rising around the perimeter of this space must have pleased Wright, for he elaborated on the concept in his house for Susan Lawrence Dana built two years later.

Even after construction, Wright continued to improve the design in his mind, and on at least several occasions was able to try his new idea. The dormer windows of the Chauncey Williams House (River Forest, 1895) were later altered — although to the delight of historians, one of the original dormers remains on the north side of the house. A building permit dates these exterior modifications as c.1900. No documentation has been found regarding the reasons for the changes, but I would submit that Wright had envisioned a better design and talked his friend and client into making the alterations. If so, his powers of persuasion must have been very great indeed.

This continual re-evaluation of a design to find an even better solution is possibly best seen in his Oak Park home, which was used as a laboratory for the twenty years he lived there (1889-1909). Rooms were added and expanded, window configurations changed and decorative elements altered.[4] In 1898 a studio was built adjoining the house and it was also in a constant state of flux. Sometimes before a particular architectural feature was incorporated into other buildings, Wright 'tried it out' in the studio; many of these were utilized afterwards, but others were discarded. He increased the ceiling heights of the rooms, altered the fireplace, moved interior partitions, and modified the entry route. The library, especially, underwent extensive changes. When first built, it had an octagonal roof that met the walls just above the windows. It was then altered with a second set of clerestory windows above the first, and the ceiling became a skylight. Next, a set of wood screens was installed in front of the upper band of clerestory windows, and finally c.1908 the second clerestory and skylight were shingled over. Wright's house and studio are currently being carefully restored to their 1909 state by the Frank Lloyd Wright Home and Studio Foundation. However, if Wright were alive today, I am certain that he would not restore the buildings to an historical date but would want to re-work them to make them fit the needs, technologies, and ideas of the 1980s!

This is perhaps best seen with the Isabel Roberts House (River Forest, 1908). In 1955 the owners of the house, a masterpiece of the Prairie years built for his secretary, asked Wright to help them with restoration of the building. Never one to look to the past, he moved forward; the result was a Frank Lloyd Wright design of the 50s. The plaster and wood-banded ceilings became lapped mahogany boards; the stucco exterior was changed to brick; the cabinets in the dining room were detailed, as the Usonians, with mahogany plywood and piano hinges. There was no attempt at a restoration; the house embodied Wright's latest innovations.

Changes for Publication

That many of the 1910 Wasmuth drawings do not exactly correspond to the buildings as they exist is well known.[5] This is due neither to a faulty memory (he was half a world away from the Midwest at the time) nor to dishonesty on Wright's part. Rather they, too, reflect the fact that his fertile mind had re-thought the designs,

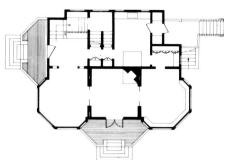

Robert Emmond House, La Grange, 1892, plan.

Warren Hickox House, Kankakee, 1900, plan.

Edwin Cheney House, Oak Park, 1904, plan.

developed improvements upon them, and updated the design for this significant publication. The windows of the Robie and Heath Houses are switched in the published version, and the Glasner House (Glencoe, 1905) is shown with a bridge and detached pavilion that were never built. The most dramatic change, however, occurred in the drawing of the W.E. Martin House (Oak Park, 1903). The volumes remained the same, but the second and third floor surfaces were drawn heavily sculpted, and the plan was elaborated with a much larger dining room. Always moving forward, Wright drew these buildings as he would have built them in 1910, were he given another opportunity.

Both Grant Manson and Henry-Russell Hitchcock have related similar incidents that occurred when doing their research. When looking through original drawings with Wright, both were aghast when the architect grabbed a pencil and began re-drawing portions of them!

Variations on a Theme

The process of development and refinement may also be seen in the designs for houses that were variations on a common theme. Since the opportunities of making alterations to a given building were few, a design was often modified and re-worked in another commission.

Development of the three-part, open living space can be seen in a line beginning with the Gale, Emmond, and Parker Houses of 1892, running through the Hickox House (Kankakee, 1900), 'A Home in a Prairie Town' published in the *Ladies' Home Journal* in 1901, and the Henderson House (Elmhurst, 1901), to the 1904 Cheney House (Oak Park). The Gale, Emmond, and Parker houses are nearly identical in plan. Designs of the 1890s, their main living spaces are only beginning to open to each other, and no attempt is made to unify them through detailing. Double doors open to a veranda from the central area. In the *Ladies' Home Journal* design and the Hickox and Henderson plans, the interior is wide open, with wood ceiling banding providing definition of the three areas. Identical in plan, the Henderson House in elevation shows great development over the Hickox

House in its unifying hip roof and in the long, horizontal appearance of the structure.

In the Cheney House this developmental line reaches its culmination. Gone are the polygonal elements of the earlier houses. The several bands of ceiling molding of the Hickox and Henderson houses have become a long series of bands, rhythmically repeated from one end of the building to the other. The placement of the fireplace in an alcove sets up a cross axis that is not present in the earlier houses, giving better definition to this space. Finally, the relation of the living room to the terrace has been increased: in the Henderson and Hickox, one door and two windows connect inside and outside; an entire wall of doors opens the Cheney House to the broad terrace.

The Barton (Buffalo, 1903), Walser (Chicago, 1903), and DeRhodes (South Bend, 1906) Houses are nearly identical in plan. In these, I believe, Wright was satisfied with the plan and was developing and refining the exterior expression of it. The handling of the brick in the Barton House is somewhat clumsy, especially at the living room windows where there is no stone lintel to support the brick above the opening and visually to span the void. Also, the presence of three materials — brick, stucco, and stone — does not provide a sense of unity to the design. In the Walser House Wright used stucco, a material more suited to the form of the building, giving it a less weighty appearance and providing a good textural contrast to the leaded glass. However, in this house the entrance is incongruous, for the detailing of the arched door does not relate it properly to the other architectural elements of the building; the additional banding of the front windows does little to help, but rather tends to put it out of scale to the rest of the building. The entrance of the DeRhodes House, with its pavilion, clerestory, and sidelights, on the other hand, is well articulated and integral to the design. With the addition of the front and rear polygonal terraces, Wright made the transition from landscape to building softer and more gradual than in the others, where it seems rather abrupt.

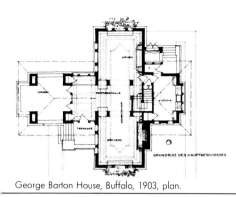

George Barton House, Buffalo, 1903, plan.

K.C. DeRhodes House, South Bend, 1906, elevation.

Frank J. Baker House, Wilmette, 1908, plan.

The DeRhodes House is clearly a better solution to the problem than is the Barton House.

Wright himself stated that the Tomek House (Riverside, 1907) was preliminary to the Robie House (Chicago, 1909).[6] The sophisticated exterior expression of receding planes found in the Robie House is missing in the Tomek, where the entrance disturbs the horizontal line of the south facade. In one sketch of the house, published recently by Taliesin in a portfolio of drawings, Wright later erased this intrusive doorway. Similarly, the living space of the Robie House shows great refinement. In both, the stairway to the raised living floor occurs in the center of the building directly behind the fireplace which defines living and dining areas; in both, space flows around both sides of this fireplace. But in the Robie House, the space also flows *through* the fireplace, and one sees the repetition of ceiling banding and light fixtures continuing beyond. It is an extremely exciting visual and spatial effect. The wall sconces of the Tomek House are replaced with a very sophisticated dual lighting system in the Robie — bright 'sunlight' comes from the exposed globes which run down the entire length of the building, while soft 'moonlight' filters down through the wooden grilles along the sides of the rooms.

In 1908 and 1909, six houses were designed which are very similar in both plan and elevation: the Davidson House (Buffalo, 1908), the Guthrie House (Sewanee, 1908, project), the Isabel Roberts House (River Forest, 1908), the Melson House (Mason City, 1908, project), the Baker House (Kenilworth, 1909), and the Steffans House (Chicago, 1909). The earliest house, the Davidson, has a two story living area, but it lacks the balcony that was added to the others. The first use of such a two story treatment is found in the 1901 design for 'A Home in a Prairie Town', published in the *Ladies' Home Journal*. Unfortunately, the last house in this developmental line was demolished in the early 1960s, so a direct comparison is no longer possible. However, from drawings and photographs, one can see that the balcony was further extended to wrap around three sides of the living

room, as the Isabel Roberts balcony began to do. The handling of the facade has also been developed further; the differentiation of planes makes the roof seem to hover over the walls beneath. The Steffans House also used art glass in abstract patterns instead of the diamond-paned design found in the others.

In 1936, with the first Jacobs House (Madison), the Usonian concept emerged. The L-shaped plan virtually eliminated the formal dining room, and each wing provided for different activities. The unique wall and heating systems were to give a very different appearance to the buildings. Two other Usonians of this type were built: the Rosenbaum House (Florence, Alabama, 1939) and the Smith House (Bloomfield Hills, 1949). A most significant improvement occurred in the Smith House in the moving of the access hall to the bedrooms to the inside of the 'L', thereby further isolating these rooms from whatever noise and activity might exist in the yard.

To Wright, these commissions with similar programs were opportunities to use an earlier solution and either explore its other possibilities or make improvements upon it, based on his ever-growing, ever-developing sense of what architecture should be. One can see definite progressions, and it is clear from the designs he chose to publish which he considered the best. On the other hand, some designs — the Beachy, Fricke, and Price (Phoenix, 1954) Houses, for example — are unique. Wright may have been dissatisfied with the result, yet realizing that a better solution was not possible, dropped that particular line of development.

Decorative Designs

A similar process can be seen in Wright's decorative designs. There are over fifteen variations of the tall-backed dining chair,[7] a form which held his attention for over sixty years. The variety is tremendous, running from the first known design, done in solid oak stock for his own 1895 dining room, to those for the Lovness House of 1955, which were fashioned of plywood. Although most of the chairs have backs with square spindles, some of

F.B. Henderson House, Elmhurst, 1901.

Walter Davidson House, Buffalo, 1908.

them have slats or solid panels instead. On some chairs, the backs run to the seat, in others to an intermediate position, and in still others they run all the way to the floor, giving the chairs an extremely architectural quality. The rear verticals are perfectly straight in some designs, on others they flare out at the bottom or taper toward the top, while on still others terminals are found. Although fewer in number, the same variation may be found in leaded glass table lamps. At first glance, several in the Dana House (Springfield, 1903) seem to be duplicated; however, closer inspection reveals that the glass patterns are really quite different. Such designs are wonderful displays of Wright's virtuosity as a designer; they show the infinite potential that a single concept can achieve. It would be difficult to say that one design is better than another, for none seems to be over- or under-developed in terms of form, proportion, or detailing. Part of the variety is due, no doubt, to Wright's goal of creating a harmony between a house and its furnishings. But part of the variety must also be ascribed to Wright's sheer love of creation.

Finally, this constant improvement of design manifested itself in his almost compulsive re-arrangement of furniture. His children tell of the hours spent moving the furniture in the Oak Park House in an attempt to achieve a better composition. Clients and owners frequently tell how, on a subsequent visit, Wright would re-arrange the furniture in their homes — often over their protests. The common explanation given is that Wright still felt the house was his to do with as he pleased. However, I would suggest that when seeing a building again after several years' absence, his mind would immediately come up with another solution, and he would want to try it. Done purely for his own information, it did not matter if anyone else looked at the new arrangement or if it was put back after he left; he still learned from it.

THE ROLE OF THE CLIENT

Throughout his life, Frank Lloyd Wright portrayed himself as the best architect of all time. Many recall Wright in the 1940s and 1950s denouncing nearly all Modern architecture and promoting himself as the possessor of a unique, truly American architectural vision. Few remember the man of the early part of the century, but I am certain that he was always positive about his abilities and about the contribution he was making to architecture. This self-image was not pure egotism on Wright's part; it was a stance necessary in order to practise his art.

Unlike a painter or sculptor who *can* (although often with much hardship) practise his art in a vacuum, the architect *must* have clients. He must sell his works of art *before* he produces them. This requires an enormous amount of faith on the part of the client — faith that can only be instilled by an architect who is confident of his own ability and can convey that confidence to the client. This is true for any architect, and for a genius like Wright, who was daring revolutionary forms and structures, it was doubly important. In committing themselves to build such structures as Fallingwater or the Johnson Wax Building, his clients had to have an unshakable belief that he was the best architect available and that his solutions, though untried, would work. This kind of confidence is not engendered by an architect who is modest and unassuming, or who tells a client that he 'thinks' a solution will be successful. The number of men and women who, in commissioning Wright, 'laid their money on the line', so to speak, is a testimony to his salesmanship and ability to market himself; the houses he built for them are a testimony to the fact that he was, indeed, the best.

The role of these clients in Wright's development as an artist cannot be overstressed. There is a great difference betwen designing and building. Although Wright had an unusual ability to visualize two-dimensional drawings as three-dimensional buildings, even he occasionally must have been surprised by the

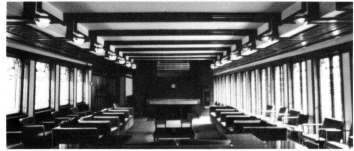

Wright dining chair. Barnsdall dining chair. Robie House, Chicago, 1909, living room.

realization of his designs. It is only in building — over and over again — that an architect can see and learn what is successful and what is not. 'Vistas of inevitable simplicity and ineffable harmonies would open, so beautiful to me that I was not only delighted, but often startled. Yes, sometimes amazed.'[8]

In the early years of his career, especially, Wright was fortunate to have so many clients willing to build his designs. As a young man in his twenties, while employed by Adler and Sullivan, he found men such as Warren McArthur, George Blossom, and Walter Gale, among others, who afforded him this essential opportunity. These 'bootlegged' houses (as Wright himself termed them), eventually led to his break with Sullivan in 1893, after which he set up his own offices. The houses built for his clients in the late 1890s are quite varied in expression, from the picturesque Chauncey Williams House (River Forest, 1895) and the Tudor design for the Nathan G. Moore House (Oak Park, 1895) to the Joseph Husser House (Chicago, 1899), with its Sullivanesque ornamentation and its forward-looking, cruciform plan and raised living quarters. Over twenty-two structures were built in the first seven years of his practice, and through this constant experimentation and re-working of form, Wright learned. A consistency of design began to emerge about 1900 — the Prairie house was born.

The Usonian house, Wright's other great contribution to residential form, had no extended period of refinement and development, yet its creation, too, depended entirely upon the fortunate combination of architect and client. Wright had long been interested in the challenge of low-cost housing, and in Herbert and Katherine Jacobs he found clients who shared his philosophy that great architecture is not necessarily beyond the means of the average American. Like the early clients, they had great faith that Wright was the best. In order to cut costs, they allowed him to simplify the house greatly, leave off many frills, and experiment with untried techniques. Their confidence also kept them from vetoing certain details, such as the brick edging of the

concrete patio, which many might have considered a needless expense, but which, as Donald Kalec has pointed out, is precisely one of the features which raise the house from the mundane to the great. Together, client and architect built an extraordinary house, ideally suited to their needs, which cost no more than had originally been budgeted.[9]

Other clients allowed Wright to show just how versatile the Usonian form was. Never becoming a formula, each design was unique. The concept was adapted to be built both on very stringent and very generous budgets. The grid became a rectangle, a square, a triangle, or a hexagon; the plan varied depending upon the site and the client's needs.[10]

In the 1940s and 1950s Wright was a highly acclaimed, though often controversial figure, and his clients came to him for a variety of reasons. None exhibited more faith than Dr. and Mrs. Isadore Zimmerman, who were drawn to Wright solely on the basis of his theories of organic architecture. Reading a published copy of his Princeton Lectures of 1930, they became convinced that he was the only architect who could build the home they wanted. Only after making this decision did they search out photographs of the buildings that are the realization of those ideals!

*   *   *   *   *

The best way to study Wright's work is not to read about it or even to read what he had to say about it, but to *look at* the buildings again and again — to compare, analyze and study them; to discover similarities and uniqueness. It is to begin one on this mission of discovery that this book is offered.

But photographs can convey only so much. True understanding and appreciation can come only by experiencing the buildings first hand. Wright's architecture is one of movement, and no photograph (mine included) can capture the exciting sense of unfolding space that comes from walking through his buildings. I urge you to experience that joy for yourselves.

Selected Bibliography

Selected Buildings

Illustrations are referenced by page number
a = above   b = below

NOTES

1. See Robert L. Sweeney, *Frank Lloyd Wright: An Annotated Bibliography* (Los Angeles: Hennessey & Ingalls, 1978).

2. Arthur Drexler, ed., *The Drawings of Frank Lloyd Wright* (New York: Horizon Press for the Museum of Modern Art, 1962).

3. See Mark David Linch, 'Ward Winfield Willits: A Client of Frank Lloyd Wright,' *The Frank Lloyd Wright Newsletter*, Vol.2, No.2, photo p.15.

4. See Donald G. Kalec and Thomas A. Heinz, *Frank Lloyd Wright Home and Studio, Oak Park, Illinois* (Oak Park: Frank Lloyd Wright Home and Studio Foundation, 1975).

5. See H. Allen Brooks, 'Frank Lloyd Wright and the Wasmuth Drawings,' *Art Bulletin*, June 1966, pp.193-202.

6. Frank Lloyd Wright, *Studies and Executed Buildings of Frank Lloyd Wright* (Palos Park, Illinois: The Prairie School Press, 1975), note to plate XXXV.

7. Tall-backed dining chairs were designed for the following buildings:
   — Own House, Oak Park, 1895 – the chairs originally had helix spindles which were later replaced with square ones
   — Husser House, Chicago, 1899
   — Bradley House, Kankakee, 1900
   — Willits House, Highland Park, 1902
   — Dana House, Springfield, 1903
   — Little House, Peoria, 1902
   — D.D. Martin House, Buffalo, 1904
   — Heath House, Buffalo, 1905
   — Beachy House, Oak Park, 1906
   — Evans House, Chicago, 1908
   — Browne's Bookstore, Chicago, 1908
   — Isabel Roberts House, River Forest, 1908
   — Boynton House, Rochester, 1908
   — Robie House, Chicago, 1909
   — Bogk House, Milwaukee, 1916
   — Allen House, Wichita, 1917
   — Barnsdall House, Los Angeles, 1919
   — Lovness House, Stillwater, 1955
   — Rayward House, New Canaan, 1955

8. Frank Lloyd Wright, *An Autobiography* (New York: Duell, Sloan & Pearce, 1943), p.147.

9. See Herbert and Katherine Jacobs, *Building with Frank Lloyd Wright* (San Francisco: Chronicle Books, 1978).

10. See John Sergeant, *Frank Lloyd Wright's Usonian Houses: The Case for Organic Architecture.* (New York: Whitney Library of Design, 1976).

Blake, Peter. *Frank Lloyd Wright: Architecture and Space.* Baltimore and Harmondsworth, Middlesex: Penguin, 1964. Biography.

Hitchcock, Henry-Russell. *In the Nature of Materials: 1887-1941, the Buildings of Frank Lloyd Wright.* New York: Duell, Sloan and Pearce, 1942. Photos of most buildings before 1941.

Manson, Grant Carpenter. *Frank Lloyd Wright to 1910: The First Golden Age.* New York: Reinhold Publishing Corporation, 1958. *The* book on the Prairie years.

Scully, Vincent, Jr. *Frank Lloyd Wright.* New York: George Braziller, Inc., 1960. Excellent introduction to Wright.

Smith, Norris Kelly. *Frank Lloyd Wright: A Study in Architectural Content.* Watkins Glen, New York: American Life Foundation, 1979. An interpretation of Wright's intentions.

Wright, Frank Lloyd. *An Autobiography.* New York: Horizon Press, 1977.

Wright, Frank Lloyd. *Frank Lloyd Wright: Writings and Buildings.* Selected by Edgar Kaufmann and Ben Raeburn. New York: Horizon Press, 1960. Wright's writings about his ideas and buildings.

Wright, Frank Lloyd. *Drawings for a Living Architecture.* New York: Published for the Bear Run Foundation Inc. and the Edgar J. Kaufmann Charitable Foundation by Horizon Press, 1959. The finest printing of Wright's drawings.

WARD W. WILLITS HOUSE, 1902
1445 Sheridan Road
Highland Park, Illinois

17   Interior, stairhall.
The juxtaposition of a very low-ceilinged entry with this soaring, two-story stairhall is very dramatic, making it one of the most exciting spaces in the house.

FRANK LLOYD WRIGHT HOUSE, 1889
428 Forest Avenue
Oak Park, Illinois

18-19   Interior, dining room.
In 1895, Wright remodeled his house, adding a playroom, a new kitchen, and this dining room. The first occasion in his own house where he designed all the furnishings, the room offers a rare opportunity to experience a complete early-Wrightian environment. The ceiling light is the first use of enclosed, indirect electric light. The room is the first project completed by the Frank Lloyd Wright Home and Studio Foundation, which is carefully restoring the building.

GALE HOUSES, 1892
Chicago Avenue
Oak Park, Illinois

20-21a   Exteriors, looking south.
All but the red house were designed by Wright for Walter H. Gale. The one on the far right was Gale's own house; the other two were built for speculation. Wright later referred to these as three of his 'bootlegged' houses, for they were independent commissions accepted while in the employ of Adler and Sullivan.

THOMAS H. GALE HOUSE, 1892
1019 Chicago Avenue
Oak Park, Illinois

20b   North elevation.
Originally built by Walter H. Gale, the house was purchased by his brother, Thomas Gale. In 1909 Mrs. Thomas H. Gale, widowed in 1907, commissioned Wright to design another house for her.

Winslow House, 1893

Roloson Apartments, 1894

Dana House, 1903

WALTER H. GALE HOUSE, 1893
1031 Chicago Avenue
Oak Park, Illinois

21b   North elevation.
The proportions of bay to dormer make this a very unique structure even in Wright's early work. The porch has recently been restored.

GEORGE W. BLOSSOM HOUSE, 1892
4858 Kenwood Avenue
Chicago, Illinois

22a   Interior, dining room.
Early in his career Wright designed a number of houses with dining rooms similar to this one, having a windowed bay at one end and either a doorway or fireplace (or both) at the opposite end. This scheme was also used by Henry Hobson Richardson for the dining room of his Glessner House built in Chicago in 1886.

WILLIAM H. WINSLOW HOUSE, 1893
Auvergne Place
River Forest, Illinois

22b   West elevation.
The front of the house is concentrated and compact. The prominent watertable, unobscured by plantings, forcefully joins the house to its site. The recent landscaping plan is faithful to the original.
23a   Detail, second story frieze, west elevation.
Sullivan's influence is seen in the abstraction of the oak leaves in this frieze of gypsum plaster. Recent information from family members indicates that the frieze may originally have been about the same color as the brick.
23b   Detail, front door.
The design of the front door, of carved oak, expresses Sullivan's idea of growth from cotyledon to oak tree.

ROBERT W. ROLOSON ROW HOUSE APARTMENTS, 1894
3213-3219 South Calumet Avenue
Chicago, Illinois

24a   West elevation.

Wright's only scheme for townhouses, these apartments were commissioned by the son-in-law of Edward C. Waller, who was involved in many of Wright's projects.
24b   Exterior detail.
The terra cotta panels are very reminiscent of Louis Sullivan's designs.

FRANCISCO TERRACE, 1895
253 North Francisco Avenue
Chicago, Illinois

25a   West elevation.
This terra cotta arch, at the entrance of the building, was removed in 1977 and placed on another building 'restoration' in Oak Park, Illinois, at Lake Street and Euclid Avenue.

ISADORE HELLER HOUSE, 1896
5132 South Woodlawn Avenue
Chicago, Illinois

25b   Exterior frieze detail, north elevation.
Executed by Richard Bock, this early design handles human figures in a very naturalistic way, and Sullivan's influence may be seen in the treatment of the plant motifs.

E. ARTHUR DAVENPORT HOUSE, 1901
559 Ashland Avenue
River Forest, Illinois

26-27   Interior, living room.
This is the last house in which Wright included an inglenook. The spherical andirons are also his design.

WILLIAM G. FRICKE HOUSE, 1901
540 Fair Oaks Avenue
Oak Park, Illinois

28a   North elevation.
This house is an interplay of horizontal and vertical planes. Two of the three tall windows are in a stairwell; the third extends through the floor of one room and into another.

FRANK W. THOMAS HOUSE, 1901
210 Forest Avenue
Oak Park, Illinois

28b   Exterior, looking southeast.
The original colors and materials, obscured for nearly fifty years, have recently been restored by the current owner.
29   Window detail.
The first floor windows of the house were executed by the Chicago firm of Giannini and Hilgart and are among Wright's finest art glass works.

SUSAN LAWRENCE DANA HOUSE, 1903
East Lawrence Avenue at 4th Street
Springfield, Illinois

30a   South elevation.
The exterior of the Dana House bespeaks its purpose — a house in which Mrs. Dana, the grande dame of Springfield society, could entertain lavishly. Wright was given an absolutely free hand in this commission, and no budget constraints existed. The decorative frieze on the second story is reminiscent of some of Wright's houses of the 1890s.
30b   Detail, entrance.
A spectacular grouping of art glass is located directly inside the front door, setting the tone for this house with its wealth of decorative designs.
31   Interior.
The two story turn-around connecting the fernery hall and the ballroom contains an intricate leaded glass lamp which is the same as those found in the dining room and a liquor cabinet with leaded glass doors.
32a   Interior.
This exquisite wall of piers and art glass doors is located between the reception area and a rear hallway. The doors, which are the finest Wright designed, were executed by the Linden Glass Company of Chicago. The fountain with its terra cotta sculpture, The Moon Children, was executed by Richard Bock.
32b   Interior, looking northeast.
Although many of the rooms in the house are two-story vertical spaces, the sense from this vantage point is of low, horizontally-flowing space.
33   Detail, art glass doors.
The art glass design for the doors in the reception area (see

Heurtley House, 1902

Cheney House, 1904

D.D. Martin House, 1904

previous page) is a stylized wisteria theme. Wright designed more art glass for the Dana House than for any other building.

ARTHUR E. HEURTLEY HOUSE, 1902
318 Forest Avenue
Oak Park, Illinois

34-35   West elevation.
Although the scale of this house is the same as the Coonley House (1908), its design is compact and concentrated like the smaller Cheney House (1904). By projecting some of the brick courses, Wright has emphasized the horizontal line of the building.
36-37   Interior, dining room.
This is the first time Wright used cove lighting. The dining chairs are recent reproductions of Wright designs.

GEORGE BARTON HOUSE, 1903
118 Summit Avenue
Buffalo, New York

38-39   East elevation.
The Barton House, commissioned by Darwin D. Martin for his daughter, was the first of the important series of Buffalo buildings. It was later incorporated into the site plan of Martin's estate, so that the Martin House (1904), the Barton House, the conservatory, pergolas, and gardens created a unified architectural expression.
40-41   Interior, dining room.
The first floor living area of the house is one large, open area with spatial definition achieved by the use of overhead decks.

EDWIN H. CHENEY HOUSE, 1904
520 North East Avenue
Oak Park, Illinois

42a   West elevation.
That Wright's Prairie houses are low, horizontal, and hug the ground may be seen very clearly here in comparison with the two story house next door.
42b   Exterior detail, west elevation.
The glass in these terrace doors is all the same, but some pieces were coated with an iridescent oxide to create a play of yellow, purple, pink, blue, and green.

DARWIN D. MARTIN HOUSE, 1904
125 Jewett Parkway
Buffalo, New York

43   South elevation and detail.
This commission was one of Wright's largest and most expensive residential projects of the Prairie years. Martin was a long time friend who helped Wright financially many times, including taking the mortgage of his Oak Park Studio in the 1920s.
44-45   Interior, dining room.
Much of the decorative detailing, such as the ceiling trim, art glass bookcase doors, and art glass windows, is missing. There is some question as to whether it was this space or the one labeled 'reception room' on the Wasmuth drawing that was actually used by the Martin family as a dining room.

WILLIAM A. GLASNER HOUSE, 1905
850 Sheridan Road
Glencoe, Illinois

46   Window detail, north elevation.
Iridescent pieces of glass are used in this design which is an abstraction of the tree of life. The three part configuration of the window is similar to the 'Chicago window' of the commercial buildings then being erected in Chicago's loop.

THOMAS P. HARDY HOUSE, 1905
1319 South Main Street
Racine, Wisconsin

47a   South elevation.
Although from the street it appears to be a two story structure, the house is actually a finely articulated three story residence overlooking Lake Michigan to the east. The living room rises two stories and is surrounded by bedrooms and balconies.

PETER A. BEACHY HOUSE, 1906
238 Forest Avenue
Oak Park, Illinois

47b   West elevation.
This is a very unusual building in many ways. The use of the multiple materials — cast stone, brick, wood and stucco — is uncommon; and the use of rough red brick, almost a clinker brick, is unprecedented. Of a very large scale, this house is

physically taller than most of his other two story structures. One explanation may be that, as Wright was in Japan at the time, much of the design and construction supervision responsibilities fell to Walter Burley Griffin, his chief draftsman. There are many similarities between this house and Griffin's Emery House of 1901 in Elmhurst, Illinois.

UNITY TEMPLE, 1906
875 Lake Street
Oak Park, Illinois

48   Exterior detail.
By designing the same piers for both the pavilions of the building, Wright was able to re-use the forms, thus keeping construction costs to a minimum.
49a   Interior, skylight.
The skylight of the temple is an example of Wright's integration of the structural and visual aspects of the building. The deep beams running north-south are solid and structural and serve to hold up the roof; the east-west members are hollow and connective, providing pattern to the ceiling.
49b   Skylight detail.
The subdued colors of the glass were used throughout the various surfaces of the temple.
50-51   Interior, temple.
By using a scheme of balconies and cloisters, Wright created a space in which every seat is close to the speaker; the minister literally has his flock gathered around him. Wright visually bends the planes around the corners and underneath the balcony. The hanging lamps are original.

EDWARD E. BOYNTON HOUSE, 1908
16 East Boulevard
Rochester, New York

52a   Interior, dining room.
This dining room still has the original furniture in it. Here for the first time Wright extends the art glass designs across multiple panels in both the ceiling light and the breakfront doors.

AVERY COONLEY HOUSE, 1908
300 Scottswood Road
Riverside, Illinois

52b   Interior.
The living room is on the second floor, and this view is across

Unity Temple, 1906

Barnsdall House, 1919

Ennis House, 1924

the stairhall into the living room. The green color on the walls is the original. Patching of the walls was in progress when this picture was taken before the 1978 fire; the area has since been restored. The wood screen above the stairway was the first of its kind in Wright's work; similar in concept to an art glass skylight, here wood framing replaces the metal caming.

MRS. THOMAS H. GALE HOUSE, 1909
6 Elizabeth Court
Oak Park, Illinois

53   Window detail.
Toward the end of his Prairie period, Wright began to simplify his art glass window designs by reducing the amount of colored glass.

KIBBEN INGALLS HOUSE, 1909
562 Keystone Avenue
River Forest, Illinois

54-55   Interior, living room.
In this late Prairie design, space flows over and under the decks that continue the line of the doorways and windows. Wright used this fireplace design again in the 1911 remodelling of the drafting room of his own office.

FREDERICK C. ROBIE HOUSE, 1909
5757 South Woodlawn Avenue
Chicago, Illinois

56-57   Interior, living room looking east.
The couch with its built-in end tables, and the two small tables in the center of the room are original to the house.

F.C. BOGK HOUSE, 1916
2420 North Terrace Avenue
Milwaukee, Wisconsin

58a   Exterior detail, west elevation.
Only 9 inches wide, the pattern of this window slit is very subtle; at first it appears to be a single pattern repeated, but closer inspection reveals two different patterns used alternately. The gold squares were produced by inserting a thin layer of gold leaf between two pieces of clear glass. The caming here is zinc.

58b   Interior, living room.
According to records now housed at the Milwaukee Art Center, this table was executed by the firm of Niedecken and Wallbridge of Milwaukee, Wisconsin.

ARTHUR RICHARDS APARTMENTS, 1916
2720-2734 West Burnham Boulevard
Milwaukee, Wisconsin

59   South elevation.
In these prefabricated buildings designed for the Arthur Richards Company, the lumber was pre-cut to be assembled into various designs. Many of these were constructed throughout the Midwest; only now are they being identified as Wright's 'American Readicut' buildings.

ALINE BARNSDALL HOUSE, 1919
'Hollyhock House'
4800 Hollywood Boulevard
Los Angeles, California

60-61   West elevation.
Although from this view Wright gives no clues to the actual scale of the building, it appears truly monumental in proportion. This house reflects an interest in Mayan architecture, as do several others of the same period.
62   Detail, west elevation.
A transitional house in Wright's work, the detailing of the Barnsdall House is similar to that of his earlier Prairie houses, but here the windows are deeply inset as protection from the bright California sun.
63   Interior detail, living room pier.
Stylization in concrete, glass, and metal ornament reflects the hollyhock motif that Aline Barnsdall chose for the house.

CHARLES ENNIS HOUSE, 1924
2607 Glendower Road
Los Angeles, California

64a   South elevation.
Prominently placed atop a hill just north of Wright's Hollyhock House, this grand residence surveys all of the Los Angeles valley to the ocean.
64b   Exterior, looking west.
The massing of the house and the textures of the concrete block give a very Mayan feeling to the building. Rather than

opening up to the light, this house is a protection from the intense southern California sun.
65   Exterior detail.
Although they do not form windows on the interior, the cut out patterns of these concrete blocks add to the textural variation.

TALIESIN, 1925
Route 23
Spring Green, Wisconsin

66-67   Interior, living room.
Since Wright continually changed his own homes, the living room at Taliesin currently reflects his last thinking concerning the building.
68a   Exterior, looking northwest.
The strong play of horizontal and vertical planes gives the house a sense of dynamism.
68b   A music stand designed for several musicians also provides light.

PAUL R. HANNA HOUSE, 1937
737 Frenchman's Way
Palo Alto, California

69   South elevation and detail.
Breaking away form the 90° floor plan, this was the first house built on hexagonal module, which Wright thought provided a more human environment.

EDGAR J. KAUFMANN HOUSE, 1936
'Fallingwater'
Bear Run, Pennsylvania

70   Exterior, south side.
The stonework of the house is laid up in an informal, naturalistic manner. In his handling of the concrete, steel, and glass, this building is perhaps Wright's answer to the Bauhaus.
71a   Interior, master bedroom.
Three-legged chairs were used throughout the house in order to provide more stability on the irregular stone floors. The Kaufmanns were great collectors of art, and much of it is exhibited in the house.
71b   Interior, bedroom.
Linens and accessories (even magazines) are changed on a regular basis in the house, so that tourists feel that the Kaufmanns have merely left for the day.

Johnson's Wax Building, 1936

Taliesin West, 1938

Annunciation Church, 1956

JOHNSON'S WAX COMPANY ADMINISTRATION BUILDING, 1936
1525 Howe Street
Racine, Wisconsin

72-73   West elevation.
This building expresses well Wright's belief that one's attention should be focused on the work at hand and not distracted by looking out of windows. The glass tubes, which unfortunately are being replaced with ripple plastic, diffused the light — and leaked.

HERBERT F. JOHNSON HOUSE, 1937
'Wingspread'
33 East Four Mile Road
Wind Point (near Racine), Wisconsin

74-75   Interior, two views of living room.
The main living space has a central fireplace core into which five different fireplaces and flues are set. One's sense of the space varies depending upon one's relation to the balcony and the fireplace.

TALIESIN WEST, 1938
Shea Boulevard
Scottsdale, Arizona

76-78   Exterior, three views looking north.
Originally the drafting room roof of this desert building was made of canvas, which kept out the wind and sand and diffused the light.

JOHN C. PEW HOUSE, 1939
3650 Mendota Drive
Shorewood Hills (near Madison), Wisconsin

79a   North elevation.
Viewed from Lake Minnetonka, the house appears as an out-cropping of stone and boards. While the occupants enjoy a view over Lake Mendota, the observer hardly sees even a window.

CARROLL ALSOP HOUSE, 1948
1907 'A' Avenue East
Oskaloosa, Iowa

79b   Exterior, looking northeast.
This house was built in two major construction stages: first, the

masonry and concrete workers put in the slab and the brickwork; the carpenters then took over and completed the building. Because the brickwork supports the woodwork, the return of the bricklayers was not necessary (as is usually the case), thus being more economical.

DAVID K. WRIGHT HOUSE, 1950
5212 East Exeter Boulevard
Phoenix, Arizona

80-81   Interior, living room.
The house for which Wright designed this carpet is based on a circular theme. Viewed from a normal angle, the colors blend for a most pleasing effect. David Wright, the third of Wright's four sons, was the first to commission a house by his father.

V.C. MORRIS GIFT SHOP, 1948
140 Maiden Lane
San Francisco, California

82   South elevation.
This project, which is a study in simplicity, was a remodeling of an existing building on a narrow alley in what was once the red light district of the city.

PRICE TOWER, 1953
N.E. 6th Street at Dewey Avenue
Bartlesville, Oklahoma

83   Exterior.
The structural system of this building is based on a tree, and, like a tree in nature, the tower appears different from every direction.

DONALD LOVNESS HOUSE, 1955
10121 83rd Street North
Stillwater, Minnesota

84-85   Interior.
This house, including all the furniture and fixtures, was constructed by the owner. As with most of Wright's work, Oriental objects are very compatible with the building.

ANNUNCIATION GREEK ORTHODOX CHURCH, 1956
North 92nd Street and West Congress Street
Wauwatosa (Milwaukee), Wisconsin

86-87   East facade.

This church is one of Wright's last buildings of reinforced concrete. The dome is supported by steel balls at the intersections of the wall to allow for expansion and contraction due to differences in temperature.
88   Exterior, looking northeast.
The entrance scale is quite deceiving, for it is much larger than it appears to be. The trellis for sunshading is very effective and is consistent with the expression of the circular motif of the building.
89   Interior.
Light fixtures illuminate the stairways in three of the four 'corners' of this circular plan. They begin at the basement, extend to the first level, and then continue uninterrupted through the balcony into the dome space.
90-91   Interior.
The vibrant interior color scheme is typical of Wright's later work. The traditional iconography of the Greek Orthodox faith has been abstracted and stylized in Wright's own way, but still conforms to the strict parameters of the church.

SOLOMON R. GUGGENHEIM MUSEUM, 1956
1071 Fifth Avenue
New York, New York

92-93   Interior.
Wright based this design on the spiral of a sea shell.

MARIN COUNTY CIVIC CENTER, 1957
North San Pedro Road at US 101
San Rafael, California

94-95   West elevation.
Wright designed the overall scheme of the buildings, and they were executed in phases by Taliesin Associated Architects after his death.

BETH SHOLOM SYNAGOGUE, 1957
Old York Road at Foxcroft Road
Elkins Park, Pennsylvania

96   West elevation.
A version of Wright's 'Steel Cathedral for a Million People' for New York City (1926), the entire building is based on the triangle, which is expressed both in plan and detail.

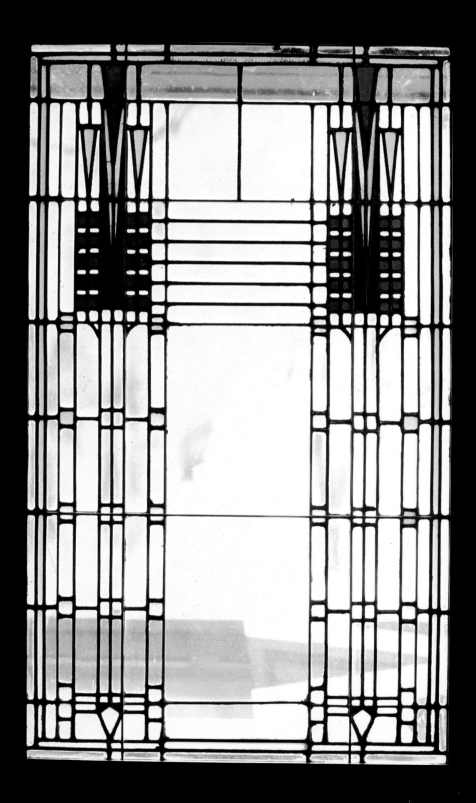

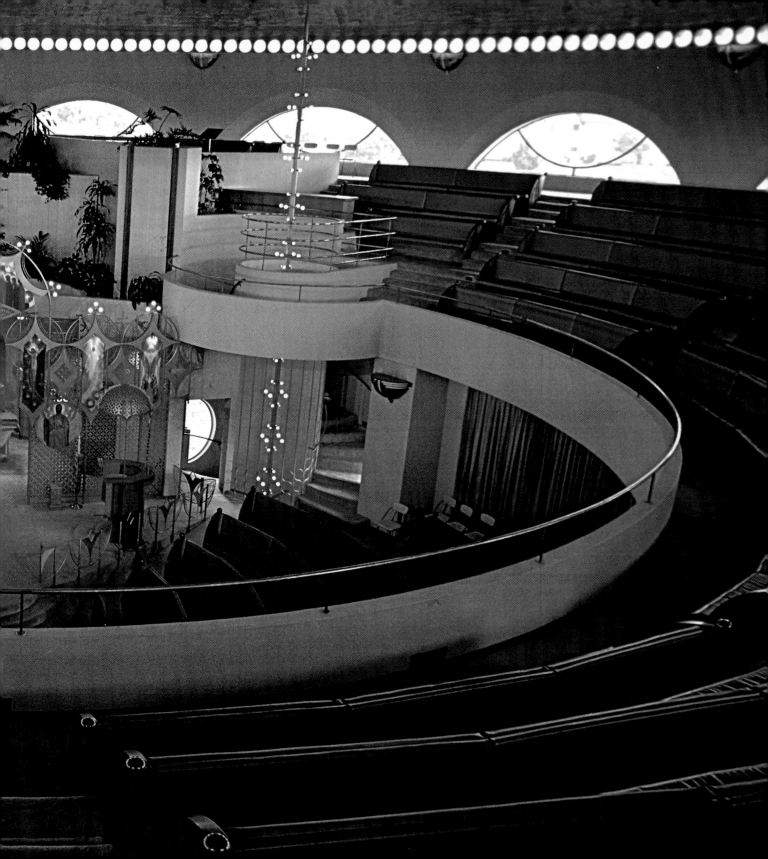